Original title:
The Verdant Versekeeper

Copyright © 2025 Creative Arts Management OÜ
All rights reserved.

Author: Adeline Fairfax
ISBN HARDBACK: 978-1-80566-732-2
ISBN PAPERBACK: 978-1-80566-861-9

Whispers of Green Canopies

In the forest where the squirrels dance,
Trees wear hats made of moss and chance.
Frogs take turns in croaky debate,
While rabbits hop like they're late for a date.

The owls hoot jokes in riddled rhyme,
Their wisdom lost to the folly of time.
Breezes giggle as they tickle the leaves,
While ants hold court in their underground thieves.

Symphony of Shaded Leaves

A symphony plays on the branches so high,
As birds mumble tunes, forget the why.
Grasshoppers dream in their midair leaps,
And caterpillars gossip while the world sleeps.

Mushrooms debate if they're veggies or not,
While turtles ponder the wisdom they've caught.
A raccoon plays maracas, tapping the ground,
As the forest's weird rhythm echoes around.

Chronicles of the Enchanted Grove

In a grove where annoyingly cheerful gnomes,
Try to pronounce their mythical homes.
Elves trip over their own shining shoes,
Laughing at trees that seem to snooze.

A bluebird sings of a funny old fate,
Where snails race quickly, but not till eight.
Bees compose jazz with a buzz that's divine,
While a grumpy old troll tries to sip on his brine.

Guardian of Flora's Secrets

A guardian stands with a comical frown,
Mixing potions while wearing a crown.
His recipes call for a dash of weird,
With ingredients that most folks have feared.

He speaks to flowers like they're old pals,
And they respond with mischievous yowls.
With mischief and magic, he keeps them in line,
In his whimsical world, where the sun loves to shine.

The Silent Echo of Blossoms

In gardens where the flowers giggle,
A daffodil tells jokes, oh so fickle.
The roses blush at puns so sly,
While daisies laugh and dance nearby.

A bumblebee buzzes with a grin,
Spreading honey like a true win.
Petals sway to a rhyming tease,
As laughter floats on the playful breeze.

Tales from the Verdant Depths

Among the blades where grass does sprawl,
Frogs recite poems, standing tall.
A chameleon tells a tale so bold,
Switching colors when the story's told.

Snails move slow, but boy, they laugh,
Their shells like shacks on a green path.
A picnic of humor that never cools,
In the woods where the wittiest critters rule.

Gossamer Whispers in the Breezy Shade

Under the trees where shadows play,
The leaves gossip in a comical way.
Squirrels perform acrobatics on high,
While cicadas chuckle as they flutter by.

With soft whispers wrapped in leafy gowns,
They mock the wanderers with playful frowns.
A breeze carries jokes from bark to bough,
Nature's stand-up, take a bow!

The Bard of the Buttercup Meadow

In a buttercup field where laughter rings,
A bard sings tales of silly things.
With butterflies that twirl and glide,
They join in, their giggles won't hide.

The dandelions sway, so carefree,
While critters cuddle up for the spree.
Every note floats on humor's wing,
In meadows where joy is the main thing.

Songs of Sylvan Serendipity

In the woods where squirrels dance,
Frogs in tuxedos take their chance.
Bunnies zoom on tiny bikes,
Chasing shadows, laughing spikes.

Trees gossip with a chuckle or two,
Sharing secrets, just me and you.
Mushrooms giggle in a row,
As sunlight tickles, watch them glow.

Birds wear hats and sing sweet tunes,
While raccoons swoon at lofty moons.
Squirrels juggle acorns high,
While bees buzz, saying, 'Oh my, oh my!'

Nature's stage, a laugh-filled scene,
Every critter plays the queen.
Amidst the green, joy finds its tune,
In this forest, we all shall swoon.

Lament of the Wisteria Bard

A bard of blooms, a tale untold,
Plucking petals, bright and bold.
Wisteria weeps for a lost tune,
While bees breakdance beneath the moon.

"Hey!" cries the vine, "Where's my hat?
I told the dragonflies to chat!
But every time I try to sing,
They steal the spotlight, oh that stinging!"

Breezes tease with whispers sweet,
While daisies tap their little feet.
The bard fluffs up in rhyme and jest,
But winds just laugh and never rest.

In tangled vines, the humor flows,
Nature's laughter—who really knows?
A concert waits under leafy arcs,
Where silence reigns and giggles spark.

Ode to the Hidden Glen

In a glen where giggles bloom,
A raccoon tries to share his room.
With a hedgehog and a tubby tortoise,
They sip on dew, feeling the nourished.

"Why so serious?" asks the hare,
Life's too short; let's shed a care!
They roll around on tufts of grass,
And through the trees, their laughter passed.

A squirrel steps in with a wobbly tail,
"Did you hear about the moose with the mail?"
The critters laugh until they wheeze,
While butterflies dip and swoop with ease.

Every corner hides a jest,
Where nature's humor is at its best.
In this glen, life's a joyful spree,
As laughter echoes, wild and free.

Secrets Woven in Leaves

In the breeze, secrets can blend,
Leaves whisper tales, pretend, pretend!
A snail confesses with a sly grin,
"My shell's too heavy; it's where I've been!"

A chorus of petals joins the fun,
As ants march proudly, one by one.
"Let's play tag!" a sparrow chirps loud,
And soon they're racing with the clouds.

A wise old oak shakes with delight,
As shadows dance in warming light.
"Why wait for rain? Let's have a laugh,
I'll tell you jokes, come take my path!"

These secrets of nature, funny and bright,
Make merry memories, day and night.
So heed the rustling, the giggling trees,
In their clever whispers, joy's a breeze.

The Poetry of Petal Winds

In a garden where daisies laugh,
A dandelion tried to draft.
It scribbled rhymes with pollen dust,
But the paper turned to mush and rust.

A butterfly, with wings of cheer,
Joined the chaos without fear.
It danced around with such delight,
As poets fled in pure fright.

A snail was stuck, in thought so deep,
Contemplating if it should leap.
Yet on its shell, a tiny quill,
Wrote sonnets slow as time could fill.

And when the sun began to set,
The blooms had secrets to be met.
They whispered tales of jest and glee,
In petals soft, wild, and free.

Sketches of a Hidden Glade

In a glade where shadows sprout,
A squirrel drew, there is no doubt.
With acorns big, it sketched away,
Creating shapes to greet the day.

A rabbit hopped up and said, 'Wow!'
'Are you an artist? Tell me how!'
The squirrel blushed, a brush in paw,
'Just don't forget to follow the law!'

A hedgehog came with colors bright,
Painting scenes in pure delight.
Yet, every stroke was met with mud,
As brushes dipped in every dud.

The sun above began to fade,
And sketches turned to an odd parade.
With laughter shared and joy intact,
They left a masterpiece, quite abstract!

Reverie in the Fern Fronds

In a thicket of ferns so green,
A curious cat was rarely seen.
It dozed and dreamed of fish and cheese,
While brushing snores through gentle breeze.

A frog, with gusto, leaped in song,
Said, 'Dear cat, you're doing it wrong!'
But the cat yawned, so wide and grand,
'These dreams are better than your band!'

A firefly blinked with glee, oh my!
It painted stars that lit the sky.
The cat then joined in fanciful sighs,
Imagining fish with twinkling eyes.

As night grew deep and shadows pranced,
The critters gathered, all entranced.
In fern fronds thick, they laughed and played,
Turning dreams to life in the glade.

The Whispering Woods

In woods where whispers touch the trees,
A chipmunk chattered with such ease.
It teased the breeze and made it dance,
While squirrels joined in a jocund prance.

A wise old owl perched up so high,
Said, 'Don't question the feathered fly!'
But a crow cawed back, with eyes aflame,
'Who needs wisdom when fun's the game?'

Around the brook, the frogs engaged,
In jokes and antics, they displayed.
With every leap came a little quack,
And laughter echoed, front to back.

As twilight fell, the fun became,
A symphony of joy, unnamed.
In the woods, both wild and cute,
The heart of nature played its lute.

The Herbarium of Heartfelt Journeys

In the garden, time does flip,
With daisies dancing, on a trip.
The roses gossip, full of flair,
While tulips tease the sun in air.

A beetle rolls a tiny ball,
Claiming turf, he thinks he's tall.
The daisies laugh, plant jokes in row,
While hidden gnomes just steal the show.

The basil winks from shaded dreams,
As marigolds weave silly schemes.
A clumsy squirrel with acorn hat,
Dances like a jumpy cat.

The moonlit nights bring playful sights,
With crickets chirping tunes of flights.
Each petal whispers silly tales,
As laughter twirls like summer gales.

Chronicles penning the Green Horizon

Under leaves where secrets dwell,
The minty whispers weave a spell.
Frogs in bow ties hop in style,
As flowers bloom and laugh awhile.

A wandering snail tells grand old tales,
Of epic quests through leafy trails.
While ants in ranks line up to cheer,
For the groundhog who's won the year.

In sunlit nooks, the nature's jest,
With mushrooms clad in polka-dress.
Each twig a story, each leaf a song,
In this green realm, we all belong.

As petals fall like funny rain,
Chasing them brings no disdain.
With dandelions in a sack,
They dare the wind to twist and crack.

Elysian Dreamers in the Thicket

In thickets thick with laughter's squeeze,
The chattering squirrels tease the trees.
With acorns tossed like silly hats,
They dance around, these clever rats.

A hedge of thyme gives sage advice,
As floral gossip rolls the dice.
Bumblebees wear goggles in flight,
Buzzing tales of the moonlit night.

The wildflowers prance, a lively crowd,
Making fun of clouds all proud.
While crickets serenade the stars,
As fireflies join with glowing jars.

Each blade of grass a ticklish tease,
Pretends to be a breeze that frees.
And in this land of leafy fun,
The stories bloom like flowers spun.

Ballad of the Flowering Fellowship

A sunflower sings with a silly grin,
Tickling petals with a chin-chin-chin.
Daffodils giggle, swaying wide,
While butterflies laugh, full of pride.

A toad in boots jumps without care,
Chasing shadows in sunlit air.
The busy bees are on a spree,
Stealing nectar, but paying a fee.

In every corner, in every nook,
Grows the laughter of an old cookbook.
Ferns flip pages, sharing a dish,
While pansies scheming make a wish.

Together they sing, a motley crew,
Composing tunes of skies so blue.
Laughter and joy, the garden's glee,
In this fellowship, wild and free.

Ephemeral Elegies of the Leaf

A leaf once told a funny joke,
It laughed so hard, it nearly broke.
The squirrel rolled, it lost its place,
In acorn dreams, it found its grace.

The wind chimed in, a gossip spree,
It whispered tales of old, you see.
While branches chuckled, roots turned red,
A dance of laughter, nature's thread.

With every flutter, tales were spun,
Of a dandelion that took to run.
It raced the breeze, with all its might,
And tangled up in a sunflower's sight.

As twilight glowed, the forest sighed,
With trees that danced and insistently pried.
For in this realm, where quirks hold sway,
Each leaf a jester, come out to play.

Melodies of the Ancient Grove

The owls were crooning, quite offbeat,
A symphony near the old oak street.
With crickets tapping in the night,
They all forgot their rightful tune, oh what a sight!

The badger wore a top hat grand,
While rabbits clapped in a merry band.
A fox conducted, all in jest,
Each note a riddle, a welcome rest.

In shadows deep, the fungi grooved,
As mushrooms bobbed, their heads they soothed.
The mossy carpet shook its head,
And giggled softly, 'Aren't we misled?'

At dawn, the forest laughed till light,
Where moonbeams danced and shadows took flight.
Together they strummed the ancient lore,
Of whimsical creatures, forever more.

Communing with the Silent Sprout

A sprout sat silent, shadows long,
It pondered deeply, a new leaf song.
Its friends were weeds, a wild surprise,
With giraffe dreams and butterfly ties.

They debated growth, how tall they'd be,
A comical vision of sprout and tree.
One wanted fame, the other cheer,
A stage of petals, a circus near.

Then came the rain, a splash, a fall,
The sprout just giggled, 'Do I start small?'
With raindrops dancing on its head,
It thought of launching a sprout-led spread.

So in the garden, they took a stance,
To sway and tumble in a growing dance.
With every touch of sun and cheer,
They followed laughter, year by year.

Rhythms of the Mossy Vale

In the vale where the moss wears shoes,
The toads tap dance, sharing good news.
A frog in shades croaks with style,
While snails race on, just taking a while.

The flowers sway to the beat of the brook,
With bees buzzing out, in every nook.
They planned a party, oh what a bash,
To celebrate spring with a fun little splash.

The old stones whispered wise, sly tricks,
As ladybugs joined with all their flicks.
The mushrooms laughed, their hats in galore,
While everyone sang of life's outdoor lore.

The rhythms echoed, a joyful call,
Where every critter had fun, one and all.
In verdant wilds, laughter is real,
A mossy vale, where we spin and wheel.

The Chronicles of the Blossoming Heart.

In the garden, flowers dance,
Wearing hats, they take a chance.
Bees are buzzing, quite the jest,
Claiming pollen, they're the best.

Butterflies on a picnic spree,
Sipping nectar, carefree glee.
A rabbit hops, a bit too fast,
Trips on petals, what a blast!

The sun tickles every leaf,
While squirrels plot some mischief.
Acorns rolling down a hill,
Chasing them is quite the thrill!

In this realm of giggles bright,
Nature's laughter, pure delight.
With a wink, the world so smart,
A symphony of joy to start.

Whispers of the Green Keeper

In the shade where secrets bloom,
A gnome whispers, 'Watch for doom!'
His garden gaffes and silly slips,
As plants giggle at his quips.

Mossy stones begin to snore,
While crickets throw a dance-off war.
Frogs in tuxedos, quite the sight,
Croaking tunes in the moonlight.

Some daisies dream of becoming stars,
While dandelions soar in jars.
'Catch me if you can!' they tease,
As breezes play among the leaves.

Every breeze a cheeky jest,
Nature's humor, never rests.
In the giggling grove so grand,
Life's a laugh, just as planned.

Lush Guardians of the Grove

Trees wear glasses, wise and old,
Telling tales that never get cold.
With roots that tickle, branches sway,
They're keeping secrets in their play.

Berries blush in twilight's glow,
As critters rush in quite a show.
Rabbits don capes, quite bizarre,
Flying off to catch a star!

With whispers soft like velvet breeze,
The flowers chat with bumblebees.
'Who's the prettiest?' they will shout,
With laughter ringing all about.

In this grove of giggling glee,
Nature laughs with you and me.
For every petal, leaf, and bough,
Is a punchline waiting right now!

Secrets in the Sylvan Shadow

In shadows deep, where giggles bloom,
Trees gossip about the moon.
A wise old owl falls off his perch,
Stumbling while he tries to search.

Mice in pajamas have a ball,
Throwing parties, making calls.
With popcorn popped and cheese galore,
They dance on leaves, who could ask for more?

A duck in slippers floats on by,
Winks at fish, says, 'Let's try!'
Underwater jokes that make sense,
In this kingdom of innocence.

With each rustle and every rust,
Nature's whimsy is a must.
In secret places, laughter swells,
Where every breeze has its own tales.

Scribe of the Emerald Canopy

In the shade, a squirrel scribbles,
With a quill made from his tail.
He writes of nuts and dodging cats,
Oh, the tales that never fail.

The rabbits gather 'round to hear,
A story of a foolhardy hare.
Who raced a leaf and lost his hat,
Now he's the talk of the woodland dare.

A wise old owl, perched so high,
Critiques the works with a beady eye.
"Your plot is thin, your twist is weak,
But at least you made me laugh and sigh!"

The forest echoes with laughter bright,
As tiny bugs join in delight.
With each whimsical tale spun anew,
Underneath the green, there's pure respite.

Chronicles of the Woodland Sage

A badger with a crooked pen,
Seeks wisdom from the trees at night.
He claims the bark has secrets deep,
But all it revealed were ants in flight.

The hedgehogs listen with a grin,
To stories of a brave, bold fox.
Who tried to outsmart a mirror pond,
And got stuck in his own paradox.

The wise old sage forgets his lines,
As critters chuckle, rolling down.
He mutters tales of slippery vines,
While wearing his old flower crown.

Yet every laugh brings joy profound,
In this leafy nook of fun and sound.
For even sages sometimes err,
But in their tales, pure joy is found.

Echoes from the Leafy Realm

Listen close to the rustling leaves,
A mischievous wind tells a joke.
A clever crow caws and weaves,
Puns of the finest oak-speak cloak.

A beetle debates with a lazy snail,
Over which way the river flows.
"I'm fast, you're slow," squeaks the snail,
"But wisdom's gained only when it grows!"

The frogs croak songs of a rainy day,
While the raccoons play hide-and-seek.
With tangled tales and silly play,
Each evening brings a brand new peak.

In this realm of laughter wild,
Every creature has a tale bestowed.
From critters small to the wise and mild,
They dance and sing down the verdant road.

Tales Beneath the Ancient Boughs

Beneath the branches thick and wide,
A turtle writes of life so slow.
He dreams of speed, yet grins with pride,
His tales spin time in gentle flow.

The chipmunks chatter, keeping score,
Of silly bets that make them laugh.
Who'll climb the tree, or roll on the floor?
They turn small tasks into a craft!

An old tree stump hosts a play,
With mushrooms as props and acorns as stars.
When the night comes, they laugh away,
While dodging the light of the fireflies' cars.

Each story ends with giggles and glee,
In the shelter of the leafy dome.
For no tale here can ever be,
Without a dash of mirth and home.

Scribe of the Verdant Silence

In leafy halls where shadows play,
A scribe once lost his way astray.
He tripped on roots while seeking pens,
And blamed the trees for all his sins.

With ink that glows like morning dew,
He laughed at squirrels in a queue.
'You write your tales with nuts,' he said,
While scribbling stories in his head.

The flowers whispered with delight,
As he penned jokes by morning light.
With every line, a chuckle brewed,
Nature chuckled, then it stewed.

So if you wander, take your care,
For trees might giggle, if they dare.
And if you hear a rustling sound,
It's just the scribe's laughter profound.

The Essence of Nature's Palette

A painter picked the hues so bright,
To splash the world with pure delight.
But as he dipped, a frog leapt high,
And turned his canvas to a pie!

The greens turned into jolly peas,
And blues transformed to buzzing bees.
His brush became a paddle, oh!
As nature giggled, putting on a show.

Each flower blushed a shade of glee,
While critters pranced with revelry.
Saintly colors danced on the breeze,
Painting laughter among the trees.

And though the artist sighed, then snorted,
He gladly joined this feast he courted.
In every stroke, a joke was shared,
Where even daisies lightly dared.

Poems Among the Whispering Pines

In ancient woods where whispers plot,
The pines conspired, or so they thought.
They found a tome of silly rhymes,
And giggled loud through quiet times.

The owls wore glasses, wise and keen,
As they read poems, quite obscene.
'Who knew the bark could tell such tales?'
They hooted back, flapping their sails.

The squirrels danced with acorns bold,
Pretending they were tales of old.
They drummed on trunks with furry paws,
As nature's audience broke the laws.

So if you hear a pine tree sigh,
Just know there's laughter passing by.
They whisper lines of joy anew,
For in the woods, the fun's for you.

The Hidden Library of Emerald

In a secret grove, a treasure lies,
With books that sparkle, oh what a prize!
The leaves are pages, the branches quill,
Each tale a giggle—what a thrill!

A rabbit read of cheese and bread,
While crickets chirped, 'No books, just spread!'
The sunbeams danced in joyful glee,
As shadows crept with a funny decree.

'Check this tale of a gassy owl!'
A tortoise grinned, bursting out loud.
They swapped their stories, giggles galore,
And left with laughter, always wanting more.

So if you wander where few have trod,
Look for the library, it's like a facade.
For every book holds a chuckle thread,
And nature's secrets, once carefully said.

Lament of the Rustling Meadows

In meadows wide, the grass does sway,
A rabbit hops and steals my hay.
The flowers nod with cheeky glee,
While bees complain about their tea.

The cows just chew and laugh away,
As I spent mine on things to say.
The sun above just grins too bright,
I lost my hat in a playful flight.

Oh, hear the wind, it whispers loud,
As I trip through a buzzing crowd.
The daisies giggle, the daisies gleam,
I stubbed my toe, or was it a dream?

So here I stand, with laughter spry,
With nature's antics that can't comply.
In meadows rustling, I will confess,
I'm but a fool in this floral mess.

Echoes of Lush Horizons

In fields so green, I like to roam,
But always find my way back home.
A squirrel waves, and then he sneaks,
To steal my snack—it's such a peak!

The clouds above are targets clear,
I holler, "Catch!" while sipping beer.
A bird replies with vocal flair,
And I just laugh, as if we care.

The trees all dance, their branches sway,
While insects hum a merry play.
The suncast shadows, perfect whisk,
But watch your step—watch out for brisk!

So join the fun, it's quite a sight,
In horizons lush, laughter ignites.
With friends so silly, let's make a cheer,
For nature's jokes are ever near!

The Keeper's Garden

In my neat rows, the veggies sprout,
But weeds are winning—there's no doubt.
The carrots dance, the tomatoes sing,
While I just search for an awful string.

The radishes are plotting, I can see,
They wink at me—how could this be?
As birds above provide the score,
They chirp my name and want some more.

Each garden gnome gives me a glare,
I tell them jokes; they seem to care.
With dirt on hands, I tip my hat,
And join the bunnies in a chat.

So under sun and moon's embrace,
The garden smiles, a funny place.
For while I toil with laughter's grace,
My veggies plot a grand disgrace!

Secrets in the Sunlight

In golden rays, the secrets hide,
The daisies gossip, side by side.
A butterfly shares tales of flight,
While snails race on in sheer delight.

The shadows play a trick or two,
As I embrace the morning dew.
The squirrels bury snacks galore,
While I wonder what's in store.

Beneath the beam, my hair's askew,
While ladybugs insist they flew.
In every corner, laughter blooms,
As mischief dances in full rooms.

With light that twinkles, bright and bold,
The secrets spill, their tales retold.
So let us laugh and dance along,
In sunlight's cheer, we all belong!

Lush Lullabies from the Grove

In the shade of leaves, whispers spread,
Where squirrels play chess and turtles are fed.
A frog croaks in jest, a wink in his leap,
As flowers giggle softly, not wanting to sleep.

While twirling and twisting, the vines find their mate,
A dandelion sneezes, it's fate, don't be late!
With petals all pink, the roses complain,
"Why bother looking fancy? It's all in vain!"

The bees hum a tune, but they usually buzz,
"Who could be sweeter? We're stingers, not fuzz!"
But nodding in rhythm, the daisies clap hands,
As breezes join in with their soft, wavy bands.

Finally twilight falls, and all takes a break,
Even the gnomes let their chuckles awake.
In this playful world, where laughter will thrive,
Who knew that the forest was so full of jive?

Lore of the Flourishing Flora

From thorns to soft leaves, their tales interlace,
Where cacti tell stories with a prickly face.
"I'm growing tall, but with patience, you'll see,
These flowers are brighter, so come sit with me!"

Come listen to berries make musical jams,
While mushrooms insist they're the world's funniest clams.
"Who can be fruity?" cries an apple in glee,
And a pear joins the chorus, "We're not just for tea!"

The ferns in the corner roll laughs in a map,
While creaky old oaks tip their branches and clap.
"Oh, youth is so fleeting!" sighs a willow so wise,
"Yet here we are dancing under wide-open skies!"

As dusk brings the laughter, the vines twist and spin,
The roots join the chorus, a rootsy din!
So gather 'round nature, for joy is the key,
In the lore of the flora, all wild and so free!

Harmonies of the Botanical Haven

In the heart of the glen, where the giggles bloom,
The daisies throw parties, but who'll sweep the room?
"Oh would you stop growing!" the violets declare,
"Your style's just a mess, it's almost unfair!"

The poppies in ruffles dance with such flair,
While peonies ponder if they should really care.
"Who wears it best? Is it me or the fern?"
"Let's settle it swiftly, I'm ready to learn!"

And just when the tune starts to rise and take flight,
A gopher pops up, in sheer joy and delight.
With a top hat and cane, he jives to the beat,
And flowers all blush, "Aren't we in for a treat?"

As dusk starts to hum with a soft, gentle tune,
The moon gives a wink, and the crickets commune.
In this botanical space where merriment stays,
The harmonies flourish in whimsical ways!

The Silent Resonance of Thicket

In thicket's embrace, the antics unfold,
With wildflowers gossiping stories untold.
"Watch out for that beetle! He's got quite the strut,
He thinks he's a king, but he's merely a rut!"

The mushrooms convene for a secretive chat,
"A snail thinks he's speedy, or so he says that!"
As roots tumble down in a loosely held race,
"Can't catch up now! It's a root-ball disgrace!"

The wispy tall grasses all wave as they cheer,
"Let's plan for a ball, but who'll bring the beer?"
"Some nectar will do!" says a clustering bee,
While thorns on the roses roll eyes and decree.

As twilight unfurls with a giggle and sigh,
The thickets all shimmer, a soft firefly sky.
In the silence that bonds this whimsical crib,
Nature's playful pulse is an unspoken rib!

Chronicles Beneath the Boughs

In the woods where squirrels plot,
They argue over nuts a lot.
The trees chuckle, leaves all sway,
While owls act as if to say.

A rabbit hops, a dance so spry,
With a top hat, oh my, oh my!
The brook gurgles, quite a tease,
As frogs croak out their melodies.

Beneath the boughs, a secret fair,
Where raccoons hold debates with flair.
Their arguments are quite absurd,
About the tastiest fallen bird.

At dusk, the fireflies take to flight,
They're disco balls, oh what a sight!
While crickets chirp in harmony,
The nightly show, a comedy.

The Sylvan Custodian

A gnome with glasses, quite the sight,
Keeps an eye on things at night.
He mumbles to the morning dew,
"Why can't you sparkle, just like you?"

The hedgehogs gossip in a row,
About the mushrooms' improper glow.
They roll their eyes, oh what a fuss,
"Who'd wear a cap as bright as us?"

The oak tree cracks a joke or two,
With branches waving, waving, woo!
The young sprouts giggle, full of glee,
"Let's play hide and seek with the bee!"

And when the moon starts shining bright,
The shadows dance, a silly sight.
With twirls and skips, they make a scene,
The forest's quirks reign supreme.

Dance of the Evergreen Spirits

In a glade where shadows grinned,
The spirits of the trees have sinned.
They twirl and leap with leafy flair,
Making all the forest stare.

A sprite named Olive sings so loud,
"Join my dance, you should be proud!"
The ferns sway, they seem to know,
They clap their hands and steal the show.

A chipmunk joins with acorn hats,
As squirrels cheer with little chats.
The party's wild, full of fun,
Even shadows join the run!

With giggles bright and laughter true,
The evergreen sings all anew.
In woods alive with nimble feet,
They'll dance until they find a seat.

Murmurs of Mossy Shadows

In the glen where shadows creep,
Mossy whispers softly seep.
The rabbits gossip in a line,
"Who stole my carrot? Oh, that swine!"

The fox prances, tail held high,
Winks at the birds soaring by.
He steals a glance, then gives a grin,
"I might just poke my nose right in!"

Toadstools plot beneath the trees,
Debating who's the best with ease.
Their tiny voices hope to climb,
They dream of fame—oh what a rhyme!

As twilight spills its golden hue,
The mossy hum begins to strew.
"Let's tell tales of silly tricks,
And how we fooled those prying pricks!"

Meadow's Quiet Narrator

In a field where daisies dance,
The cows all dream of dairy chance.
A ladybug is having tea,
With ants who claim, "Come sit with me!"

The grasshoppers sing off-key,
As squirrels throw nuts like confetti.
A rabbit hops, all tangled up,
In a stream of dandelion fluff.

The sun winks down—a golden jest,
While butterflies put on their best.
A bumblebee with pompous flair,
Complains, "My pollen isn't fair!"

So laugh, dear friend, join nature's spree,
Where all is fun and wild and free!
The meadow speaks with giggles bright,
Each creature's tale, a sheer delight!

Verses from the Emerald Expanse

In the woods where tales are spun,
A frog insists he's also fun.
He croaks a beat, the mushrooms sway,
While fireflies dance, so bright, so gay.

The owl, wise, shakes its head in glee,
As raccoons plot from every tree.
"Sneak in the night!" they whisper low,
To raid the picnic down below.

The chattering squirrels, oh what a sight,
Playing acorns like a game of fright.
They hoard their snacks, but what a tease!
They drop a nut—"Oops! Whoopsie, please!"

But echoing laughter, wide and loud,
Brings joy to every leafy crowd.
In this expanse of glee, you'll find,
Nature's jesters—oh so kind!

Tales of the Canopy Haven

Beneath the leaves, a gossip spreads,
Of tiny foxes tucked in beds.
They swap their dreams of running swift,
And share a secret, furry gift.

The raccoons wear their masks with pride,
In moonlight's glow, they sneak and glide.
With giggles, they dance down the lane,
Not thinking once of winter's bane.

A chipmunk's caper steals the show,
With twitching tail and flair, oh whoa!
He says, "I'm sleek, I'm fast, I'm bold,
Just don't ask me to be controlled!"

The canopy whispers, "Shh, be light!"
As creatures giggle throughout the night.
With every tale that climbs the trees,
The world is full of joyful tease!

Rhapsody of the Woodland Chronicle

In a glade where mischief brews,
A squirrel claims it lost its shoes.
A wise old turtle rolls his eyes,
And chuckles deep—'Oh what a surprise!'

The ferns stuck out their leafy tongues,
While chatting wildly in their songs.
"Oh stop it, please!" a near tree moans,
As giggles whirl with happy tones.

The fox prances, showing off his flair,
With every leap, he snags the air.
A dance-off starts beneath the moon,
With fluffy bunnies out of tune.

So gather round, listen and see,
These woodland tales are wild and free!
With every chuckle, leap, or grin,
The chronicles of fun begin!

The Symphony of Rooted Lives

In a garden of chatter, the roots all convene,
One claims to know secrets, but knows not what they mean.
The daisies are giggling, their petals a-fluff,
While the carrots are whispering, 'Enough is enough!'

The radishes wobble, they dance with such style,
The broccoli nods, all green and in denial.
Yet the peas keep on rolling, all round and so bold,
Laughing at tales that the lettuce has told!

The worms make a symphony deep underground,
With solos and duets, a squirmy sound.
While the cacti just chuckle, so prickly and tough,
They say, 'Life's a desert, and that's just enough!'

So let's raise a toast to this quirky brigade,
Each root a fine actor, in nature's parade.
With a sprinkle of humor, and laughter so rife,
We'll celebrate joy in this tangled-up life!

Tales from the Thickets

In the heart of the thicket, where shadows abound,
A squirrel spins stories, with leaps and with bounds.
The branches all listen, with twigs all a-twitch,
As pines make a chorus, their needles a-pinch.

The mushrooms are gossiping, weaving a plot,
'Is that a bear snoozing? Well, maybe it's not!'
The raccoons are plotting, with masks on their face,
'A heist of the berries would be quite the chase!'

The owls hoot in laughter, folks say they're so wise,
Yet who's been hoarding the best blueberry pies?
The frogs croak a melody, ribbiting in time,
While the crickets all chirp a buggy old rhyme.

Amidst all the chatter, a wise turtle sighs,
'Quiet down now, friends, you're hearing my cries!'
But with laughter erupting, the thickets will sway,
With tales spinning freely, we'll love the old way!

Marvels of Verdurous Realms

In realms lush and verdant, where laughter runs free,
A cabbage confesses, 'I'm smarter than me!'
The flowers they flourish, in colors so bright,
Saying, 'Follow my lead, from morning till night!'

The bushes are boasting, they've grown quite a crop,
While the turnips are plotting the ultimate flop.
The sunflowers waltz in the bright sunny glow,
As daisies proclaim, 'We put on quite the show!'

A chipmunk takes center stage with a shout,
'Please be in my fan club, we'll go on a route!'
But the oak tree just chuckles, its trunk all a-twitch,
'Just be careful, dear friend, or you might hit a hitch!'

So dance with the dreamers in this vibrant field,
Where every green sprout has a secret to yield.
Let's share all our laughter, and free up the seams,
For life's just a circus, or so it seems!

Harmonies of the Flourishing Fields

In fields of bright wonder, where mischief does bloom,
The critters all gather, to banish the gloom.
The corn sings a tune, swaying left and right,
While the daisies declare, 'We'll party all night!'

The bees buzz in rhythm, a vibrant parade,
Sporting tiny top hats, all dressed for the raid.
The rabbits are plotting, a chase through the hay,
While the thistles are waiting to join in the play!

The wind is a joker, it tickles the trees,
As tumbleweeds tumble, with giggles and wheezes.
Each petal a dancer, each stalk a bright dream,
In the playful arena, they all form a team.

So gather your chuckles, your smiles and cheer,
In fields full of wonders, there's nothing to fear.
For laughter's the harvest, we'll reap and we'll sow,
In this land of abundance, where joy's sure to grow!

The Greenkeep's Charms and Whims

In a garden where gnomes giggle,
Mischief dances with every wiggle.
The daisies debate in a flowery chat,
While a squirrel swipes snacks like a chubby brat.

With each rainbow, the colors collide,
A butterfly flutters, a squirrel takes pride.
The roses wear hats, quite silly and bright,
While the carrots hum tunes in the soft twilight.

But be sure to watch the carrot brigade,
They'll dance on your toes as if unafraid.
With twirls and with hops, they'll prance all around,
And leave you bewildered, lost in the sound.

So if you happen to roam through this land,
Just laugh with the weeds; take a quirky stand.
For nature's pure whimsy, with humor relayed,
Turns any lush garden into a parade.

Twilight Tales of the Leafy Avatar

When shadows stretch long and the sun gives a wink,
The trees start to gossip, their branches all link.
The mushrooms hold court, each one dressed to impress,
With their polka-dot caps, they aim to distress!

Crickets begin their evening concerto,
While fireflies twirl in a lightning-like flow.
The owls read the stars, hooting jokes by the score,
While the wind cracks a smile and flutters the door.

Under twinkling lights, the bunnies debate,
Who's the fastest of all in their critter-like fate.
The hedgehogs roll dice in a game quite absurd,
Trying to score with the best supper word.

So linger a moment in this twilight scene,
Where laughter and nature make a jovial team.
In moonbeams and shadows, the laughter spills free,
In leafy conversations, oh what glee there'll be!

Songs of the Overgrown Soliloquy

In jungles untamed, where the vines intertwine,
A parrot recites quite the humorous line.
Frogs croak their wisdom, quite comically crude,
As the sages of moss gather round for some food.

The sun tickles leaves with a golden embrace,
While the turtles get silly in a slow-motion race.
With giggles from flowers and snickers from trees,
The wind plays a tune that puts everyone at ease.

Bananas wear wigs while the mangoes hold court,
As the avocado moon starts to gently cavort.
The berries all chatter, sharing juicy good cheer,
While the shadows dance lightly, with nothing to fear.

So join in the jest on this mirthful spree,
Where nature's own laughter is wild and free.
In the heart of this green, where the silly things sway,
A song of delight paves the bright, leafy way.

The Nature's Narrative Keeper

In a forest where fables and giggles entwine,
The trees tell their tales with a funny design.
No whisper too soft, no joke too absurd,
As a chipmunk does stand-up, his punchlines unheard.

The brook starts to babble, adding lines to the song,
While butterflies flit, laughing all along.
The flowers roll laughter, petals in glee,
As the sunset joins in with a warm jubilee.

Bears in top hats attend nature's grand ball,
With the bunnies providing the waltz for them all.
Each leaf has a story, each twig has a quirk,
Entwining the laughter that nature can work.

So gather your friends for this narrative spree,
Where every bright bloom holds a jest or a key.
In the heart of the woods, where the fun never ends,
Nature's wild tales are the quirkiest friends.

Notes from the Rustling Fern

In the forest, frogs play chess,
One hops in, and causes a mess.
Leaves giggle when the wind rushes,
Swaying like a dance, oh, how it blushes!

Squirrels in coats, with nuts to share,
Argue who has the fluffiest hair.
The owl hoots a joke, so wise and sly,
While raccoons just roll their sleepy eyes.

A beetle struts, with a crown on its head,
Claiming the title, "Duke of the Dead!"
But the ants just laugh, they're under his reign,
Planning a parade, it's their time to gain!

So take a stroll where the wild things grow,
Join the fun, let your worries go.
In this backyard, laughter is free,
The universe smiles, beneath the old tree.

Poetry of the Emerald Arbour

The trees in green, they write their verse,
Filling the air, with laughter diverse.
A sneezy pine, with its cones galore,
Sneezes out rhymes, that leave us wanting more!

In the thickets, a badger recites,
His sonnets of snacks and nocturnal delights.
Birds chirp back in harmonized tunes,
Quoting the sun, and waxing the moons.

There's a squirrel with a tale of snacks,
While rabbits provide great comic acts.
Nature's stage, a whimsical scene,
Where giggles bloom, on petals of green.

Leaves fall like confetti, in a swirl and twirl,
As butterflies tease and swirl in a whirl.
Gather for laughter, in nature's grand show,
Where every creature puts on a glow!

Legacies of the Flora Keeper

In a garden of giggles, where flowers play,
Thorns tell tales on a bright sunny day.
Roses gossip, with petals all prim,
While daisies laugh, they will not be grim.

A caterpillar's dream, to be a lovely moth,
Every week he measures, the fabric of 'broth'.
With a wink and a smile, he spins a cocoon,
Crafting an outfit, to dance under the moon.

The funny old willow leans low just to peek,
As a snail flips pancakes, 'Oh what a week!'
Turtles enjoy stories 'neath shady trees,
Chortling with toads, while sipping on breeze.

Life in green hues, is fun-filled and bright,
Under the sun's grin, everything feels right.
So come outside, let's sip from the cup,
Of joy in the leaves, as the sun's coming up!

The Keeper of Nature's Chronicle

In shadowy glades, the critters convene,
To share in their tales, what a curious scene!
A gopher recites, with popcorn in hand,
The gossip of trees across the wide land.

A chattering crow boasts of riches untold,
While a hedgehog giggles, "I'm spiky, not bold!"
With mushrooms for chairs, they settle and jest,
Chasing away all the woes that they've guessed.

Butterfly ballads drift soft on the breeze,
As flowers nod gently, with grace and with ease.
"Join us!" they sing, "to the banquet of fun,
Where every small creature is loved 'neath the sun!"

So pen down the antics of flora so grand,
In a realm where laughter dances on land.
For nature's a keeper of tales loud and spry,
Whispered in giggles, beneath the blue sky!

Revelations of the Leafy Manuscript

In a book made of leaves, oh what a sight,
Squirrels debate if acorns taste right.
A page turns with flutter, the critters now cheer,
For a plot about nuts that draws them all near.

The pages are crinkled, the ink's made of sap,
Birds circle above, each getting a map.
They find hidden treasures in forgotten groves,
But the best ones are just where the wild onion grows.

A frog writes a chapter in a splashy green pen,
While raccoons conspire, "Let's do it again!"
Their laughter rings out through the trunk and the vine,
As they scribble their fun, oh the joy is divine!

Legacies Under the Cedar's Limbs

Beneath the great cedar, tales spark in the air,
With owls hooting loudly, giving wisdom to share.
The shadows hold secrets, like pranks from the past,
As critters invent legends, too funny to last.

A chipmunk claims glory for a nutty heist,
While the bunnies all giggle at his unlikely tryst.
Reflecting on follies, each character's flare,
Leaves giggle on branches, light dance everywhere.

The wise old raccoon bats a gnarled eye,
"Remember the time when we all learned to fly?"
They chuckle and chortle, what fun, what a mess,
Under cedar's shadow, it's pure happiness.

The Whispered Tales of the Forest Guard

In the hush of the woods, tales burst forth with glee,
Of flora and fauna, all singing like three.
A hedgehog recites in a voice somewhat squeaky,
While the fox plays guitar, quite chipper and cheeky.

"Once I wore pants made of leaves!" he does brag,
While the rabbits fall over, they laugh 'til they sag.
Another tall tale of a snail's epic race,
Leaves creak from the chuckling, what mirth fills the space!

As shadows grow longer and dusk starts to creep,
They spin yarns that send every creature to sleep.
Yet the laughter still lingers, like echoes of song,
In the heart of the forest, where all can belong.

Echoing Dreams from the Green Domain

In dreams of the green, where the giggles take flight,
The mushrooms conspire, conjoined in delight.
With whispers of sunlight, they dance on the breeze,
To a tune only they know, brought forth by the trees.

The rabbits hold court, in a leafy throne chair,
Debating the silliest, craziest fare.
"Who'd win in a race, a turtle or me?"
Explosive with laughter, they answer with glee!

The fireflies twinkle, composing their song,
"We'll draw the stars closer—come join us, it's wrong!"
The earth chuckles softly, and so do the streams,
In the echoing night, it's a world full of dreams.

Fables of the Flourishing Earth

Once a worm wore a tiny hat,
He danced with a slug to a jazzy spat.
They twirled through the mud, what a sight!
Who knew earthworms had moves so bright?

A beetle thought he could sing like a star,
But a grasshopper laughed, said, "Not by far!"
They formed a band, oh what a show!
Till raindrops fell, and they ran to the crow.

The daisies joined in for a wild tea,
With cups made of petals, oh what glee!
But the honeybee buzzed, "Where's my snack?"
And the bumblebee said, "You can't have my pack!"

So here's to the critters, jazzy and bold,
In stories of nature, forever retold.
Their fun in the dirt, oh how they thrive!
A fable of laughter, where all come alive!

Sonnet of the Saturated Soil

In gardens of goo where the puddles splash,
A mole in a raincoat made quite a dash.
He slipped on a worm, doing the worm dance,
And shouted, "My friend, you must take this chance!"

The beans in their row started to sway,
Singing to squashes, what a bright day!
But the carrots complained, "We are under a flood!"
"At least we aren't squished in a muddy old bud!"

A radish then teased them, "Why fret and mope?"
"We've got sunshine and dreams; it's not all a slope!"
So they laughed and they played, what a sight to see,
In tales where the soil holds such humorously glee.

With roots all entwined, and leaves in the air,
Each veggie giggles 'neath the sun's warm glare.
So here's to the soil, muddy but bright,
Where plants spin their fables from morning to night!

Memories Among the Wildflowers

Once a daisy dreamed of being a cake,
And asked the sun for a sprinkle to make.
But the wind just chuckled, "You're sweet as can be!"
"A cake made of flowers? That's laughter for me!"

Then a lily chimed in, "Let's throw a big bash!
With honey as frosting, oh what a splash!"
They invited the bees, and a bashful old snail,
Creating balloon flowers with vines as the trail.

The poppies wore hats made of fluff and of dew,
While the violets danced, in sparkly blue.
Yet the thistle stood grumpy, "What's all this fuss?
You want to wear pollen? You're all making a fuss!"

But the flowers all laughed in the soft summer glow,
Getting tangled in laughter, it started to flow.
So here's to the blooms hiding joy in their hearts,
In memories bright where the laughter imparts!

Dreams Woven with Ivy

An ivy once dreamt of becoming a hat,
But a squirrel just teased, "You're better than that!"
So she twirled around trees in a leafy parade,
While the oak laughed aloud, "You're the best of the shade!"

With tendrils quite clever, she climbed and she climbed,
In a garden where laughter is sweetly entwined.
A frog on a lily croaked out a tune,
"Your dreams are as wild as a dance with the moon!"

The daisies all tagged along in a row,
Wearing vines like necklaces, putting on a show.
A party of green where giggles unfold,
In a world of fine ivy, where stories are told.

So let's raise our glasses to dreams that take flight,
To wild little wishes twinkling at night.
For ivy knows well, when you laugh, you can climb,
In a garden of joy, through the rhythms of time!

The Canopy's Lyricist

In the shade of trees so green,
A squirrel dances, nimble and keen,
With acorns as hats, a grand masquerade,
While birds cheer loudly, a joyful parade.

The breeze whispers jokes, oh what a tease,
As flowers giggle, tickled by leaves,
A butterfly trips, in a fluttering spin,
Leaving the ants laughing, their patience worn thin.

Beneath the branches, the laughter grows,
Where frogs jump in sync, stealing the show,
With every ribbit, they croak a new tune,
Creating a symphony under the moon.

Night falls softly, stars take their cue,
The moon pulls a prank with a bright balloon,
As owls hoot puns in the cool of the night,
In this leafy realm, everything feels right.

Glimpses of Nature's Storyteller

In a meadow of giggles, the daisies sway,
While butterflies gossip, in bright array,
With petals as pages, they share their tales,
While bees buzz along with their sweet, sticky trails.

A chubby old toad croaks a loud verse,
As dragonflies dance, oh what a universe!
With winks and a wiggle, they flirt with the sun,
In this vibrant realm, the jokes never run.

Rabbits leap high, with top hats and flair,
Throwing a party without a care,
Their carrot confetti fills up the air,
And all of the critters join in with a pair!

As dusk draws near, the laughter won't cease,
With fireflies glowing, they throw a grand feast,
In the heart of the wood, where legends unfold,
Every day is a story, each moment retold.

Breaths of the Wild Sanctuary

In a forest where squirrels convene,
They plot mischief, if you know what I mean.
With acorns flying, they take their aim,
While raccoons giggle, it's quite a game.

A butterfly dances, wearing a hat,
Chasing a bee, oh, what's up with that?
They stir up the leaves; they twirl and spin,
This chaotic ballet, let the fun begin!

Frogs serenade from their lily pad throne,
While the turtles argue, "Hey, leave my stone!"
And crickets offer their runs as a band,
Creating a concert, all unplanned!

In this wild sanctuary, wacky and bright,
Every critter joins in, bringing pure delight.
A world filled with laughter, so vivid and wild,
Nature's playground, where chaos is mild.

Chronicles of Nature's Palette

A canvas of green, where the oddest things grow,
Like carrots in pajamas, giving quite a show.
They wiggle and giggle beneath the ground,
Sprouting some laughter, joy all around.

The daisies wear spectacles, oh what a sight!
While sunflowers gossip about the moonlight.
They chat about bees and their fuzzy ballet,
In this quirky garden, they frolic and play.

The tomatoes debate, are they fruits or are they?
With peppers insisting, "Just spice up your day!"
Together they form a salad of fun,
In the lively kitchen, the laughter just spun!

A gallery painted with nature's own brush,
It's a spectacle grand, not some hurried hush.
Here each leaf gives a wink, sunny and bright,
In the chronicles of growth, there's sheer delight!

The Anthology of Leaf and Branch

Beneath the branches, where the shadows play,
A squirrel commissions a dance every day.
With a flip and a twist, he steals the show,
But ends with a tumble, oh dear, oh no!

A wise old owl hoots with a chuckle and grin,
As rabbits join in with a jitterbug spin.
Grasshoppers join, all hopping about,
While the shy little ferns peek, giggling out.

The trees share tall tales of their lofty loot,
Like the time they were mistaken for super cute root.
With every snicker, they sway to the beat,
In this leafy anthology, life's quite a treat!

Each branch has a story, each leaf has a laugh,
In this merry forest, we dance and we quaff.
A community thriving, where joy is the stance,
In the anthology of nature, let's all take a chance!

Murmurs from the Flourishing Backwoods

In the backwoods where whispers grow tall,
The trees take bets on who'll tumble and fall.
With roots all entwined and leaves that would sway,
Every rustle holds secrets of hilarity's play.

Chipmunks on scooters zip past with a cheer,
While owls drop "knowledge" with one flappy ear.
The turtles applaud from their slow-paced parade,
Saying, "This life's too funny, let's seize the day!"

With mushrooms that giggle and shadows that dance,
This woodland is known for its wild circumstance.
Each critter a character in the grand scheme,
Murmurs of laughter, as bright as a dream.

A chorus of chuckles fills up the night air,
From frolicking fauna, it's joy everywhere.
In the flourishing backwoods, mischief abounds,
In the kingdom of humor, it's fun that surrounds!

Treasures from the Flora Archives

In a garden deep, where plants do grin,
Lydia found a gnome, sporting a spin.
He traded her secrets, of thyme and vine,
For a scoop of ice cream, oh how divine!

Petunias giggled, their petals a-flutter,
While daisies whispered, "We just love butter!"
A sunflower wore a bright, silly hat,
It danced in the breeze, waving to a cat!

With herbs that could talk, each one in a jest,
Chives gave a wink, while parsley confessed.
"Life's but a play in a soil-made stew,"
Said the carrots who dreamt of a theatrical crew!

Lydia laughed as she skipped with delight,
In a world of green chuckles, everything's bright.
Among silly blooms where laughter takes flight,
She found every treasure stitched into light!

The Voice Beneath the Verdant Vault

Beneath the leaves, there's a croaking croon,
A frog claims the throne, 'I'm the king of the moon!'
With jokes about flies, he sings with such glee,
His royal audience? A crowd of three bees.

Old roots hold stories, of mischief and cheer,
A wise oak chuckles, "I'm glad you are here!"
"Saplings, take note, be humble and kind,
Unless an acorn rolls—you'll soon be confined!"

The vines twist and twirl, in a dance full of fun,
While dandelions cheer on a bright summer run.
Caterpillars giggle, draped on their leaves,
In the tales of the vault, it's laughter that weaves!

With roots that hold secrets, green laughter will call,
Every leaf has a joke ready for all.
From gnarled, ancient branches, to sprouts that are tough,
In a world where whispers are all just enough!

Shadows of the Verdure Patron

In the shade of a tree with a face that could grin,
Lurked a squirrel who chattered—'Come join in my din!'

He'd hoard all the acorns, proclaiming his quest,
For the world's nuttiest record, he claimed to be best!

Under the branches, with shadows that laugh,
The bluejay chortled, "Do you follow my path?"
"Just skip over puddles, and don't grab a snack,
'Cause I heard it's a trap when you bend for a pack!"

Each rustle of leaves held a giggle or two,
As chipmunks discussed their grand plans for a stew.
"Let's mix in some berries, with a splash of fresh rain,
And hope our dear patrons don't think it's all plain!"

So shadows grew tall, in a play of delight,
With critters uniting in a whimsical fight.
For nature's thick curtains held laughter so clear,
In the heart of the woods, joy reigned without fear!

Poems of Bloom and Bough

Each bloom held a story, a giggle or two,
Roses debated, while lilacs just knew.
"What's the fuss with the thorns?" asked the bold daffodil,

"Do flowers get snappy or just seek goodwill?"

A tulip chimed in, with a colorful flair,
"Let's swap all our petals, and show off our hair!"
Wildflowers laughed, as they painted the glen,
While bees buzzed along, crafting rhymes with a pen.

"Let's bloom into laughter, with smiles that can shine,
For nature's our muse, and creation's just fine!"
Said the poppies at dusk, with their threads spinning tight,

As the evening drew near, glowing flowers took flight.

So gather all blooms, from the big to the wee,
In this garden of whimsy, where joy's always free.
Their verses, like petals, drift soft on the air,
In a dance of sweet laughter, which we all can share!

www.ingramcontent.com/pod-product-compliance
Lightning Source LLC
Chambersburg PA
CBHW071826160426
43209CB00003B/215